Berklee

In the Pocket

SINGER'S
Handbook

T0082048

Anne Peckham

Berklee Media

Vice President: Dave Kusek
Dean of Continuing Education: Debbie Cavalier
Business Manager: Linda Chady Chase
Technology Manager: Mike Serio
Marketing Manager, Berkleemusic: Barry Kelly
Senior Graphic Designer: David Ehlers

Berklee Press

Senior Writer/Editor: Jonathan Feist
Writer/Editor: Susan Gedutis Lindsay
Production Manager: Shawn Girsberger
Marketing Manager, Berklee Press: Jennifer Rassler
Product Marketing Manager: David Goldberg

ISBN 978-0-87639-057-3

Berklee
Press

1140 Boylston Street
Boston, MA 02215-3693 USA
(617) 747-2146

Visit Berklee Press Online at
www.berkleepress.com

DISTRIBUTED BY

HAL•LEONARD®
CORPORATION
7777 W. BLUEMOUND RD. P.O. BOX 13819
MILWAUKEE, WISCONSIN 53213

Visit Hal Leonard Online at
www.halleonard.com

Printed in the United States of America by Patterson Printing
11 10 09 08 07 06 05 04   5 4 3 2 1

Contents

Introduction to Practicing

Practicing helps you internalize and perfect techniques. You can use practice sessions to learn new tunes, strengthen your voice, extend your breath support, clarify diction, and fine-tune all aspects of your singing.

Practice sessions should be no more than one hour in length. Other instrumentalists, such as guitarists or pianists, may be able to practice for hours without problems. However, vocal cords can tire more easily, especially in young or inexperienced singers. Practicing for long periods of time, and at random, infrequent intervals, can reinforce old bad habits and create new problems. Because of this, singers should practice four to six days a week, for thirty to sixty minutes at a time.

If you miss your practice sessions, don't become discouraged. Get back in the swing of things and pick up where you can. Improve and freshen your practice routine, to keep yourself from becoming bored. When you are training, it is best to be consistent, so don't become discouraged if you have setbacks. Move ahead with renewed commitment.

Plan to rehearse several times well in advance of a performance. This way, you can avoid vocal burnout and become completely comfortable with your music before a performance. It will also give you a comfort level that helps you feel more prepared and less anxious about performances. Feeling well prepared goes a long way toward staving off stage fright and nervousness.

Breath Management

Your voice is a wind instrument that needs breath to produce sound. Training your body and unconscious mind to manage the breathing process will give you the control you need to sing longer phrases, to sing high and low notes well, and to gain better control over dynamics.

Correct and Incorrect Posture

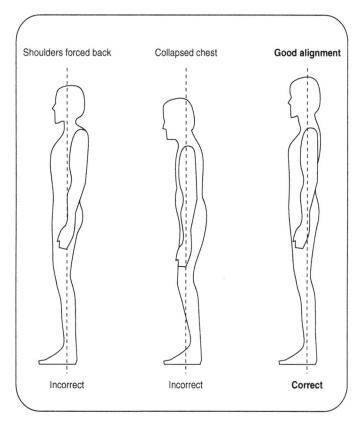

Shoulders forced back   Collapsed chest   **Good alignment**

Incorrect   Incorrect   **Correct**

To establish good posture, start with a comfortably high chest, relaxed knees (not locked), and feet hip-distance apart. As you become familiar with good posture, it will feel more natural to you. During singing, be sure to keep your chest comfortably high. Try practicing while standing in front of a mirror. It may be easier to see good posture than to feel it.

Inhalation and Exhalation

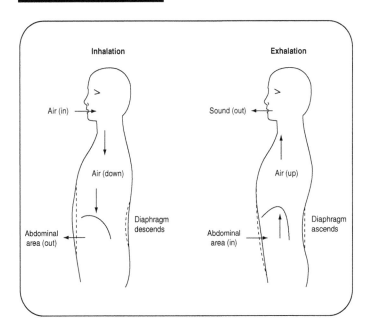

Four Steps to Effective Breathing

Try this simple exercise that outlines four steps of the breathing process.

1. Stand with your body aligned, your feet hip-distance apart, and your chest comfortably high.
2. Inhale through your nose and mouth by expanding around your waistline and relaxing your lower abdominal muscles.
3. Allow your lower abdominal muscles to contract slightly, as you start to sing a long tone in the middle of your range.
4. Maintain your comfortably high chest position, and keep your ribs open, as you sing. Don't let your chest collapse.

When inhaling, don't overfill your lungs. Stuffing your lungs creates tension in your throat and jaw before you even make a sound. Inhale completely by expanding around your waistline and in your lower abdominal area, taking care not to create tension by lifting your shoulders.

The Diaphragm

The diaphragm is a flat muscle, curved in a double-dome shape, separating the chest cavity from the abdominal cavity. It connects to the bottom of your ribs and is the floor of your rib cage.

Diaphragm Inhalation and Exhalation

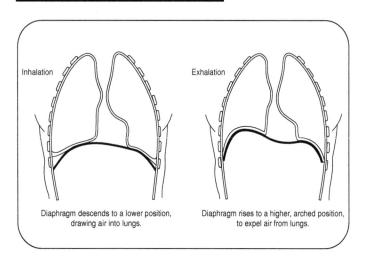

Inhalation

Exhalation

Diaphragm descends to a lower position, drawing air into lungs.

Diaphragm rises to a higher, arched position, to expel air from lungs.

Ribs and Lungs

Your rib cage is comprised of bone and cartilage. During breathing, the attached muscles open and close your rib cage, filling and emptying your lungs. When you sing, steady flow of air to your vocal cords is achieved by opening your ribs and slightly contracting your abdominal muscles.

This exercise will help increase your awareness of the expansion of your rib cage.

1. Place your fists on your sides above your waist.
2. Take a full breath, and feel the expansion of your rib cage.
3. Exhale, and feel your rib cage become narrow.
4. Take a second breath, spreading your ribs as wide as you can. Don't lift your shoulders.
5. Hold your breath but keep your throat open. Slowly, count to four. Maintain an open rib cage as you hold your breath. You will feel the external intercostal muscles of your ribs working to stay open.
6. Exhale, and allow your rib cage to become narrow again.

The Abdominal Muscles

These powerful muscles cover the entire abdominal region, running vertically and diagonally across your belly. Your lower abdominal muscles relax outward during inhalation and contract inward slightly during exhalation.

During singing, your rib cage should stay open while your abdominal muscles move in slightly. This is called support; it enables your diaphragm to ascend to its high position at a slower rate, allowing you to sustain longer phrases and maintain better pitch control. If your ribs descend immediately, air will rush out too quickly for good phrasing, or a breathy tone may result. Collapsing your ribs and chest tightens your neck and throat muscles, preventing your larynx from functioning freely. This can cause your singing to sound and feel constricted. Good abdominal support will help you keep your neck and throat relaxed, bringing you a full and resonant tone.

Collapsed Chest and Open Chest Postures

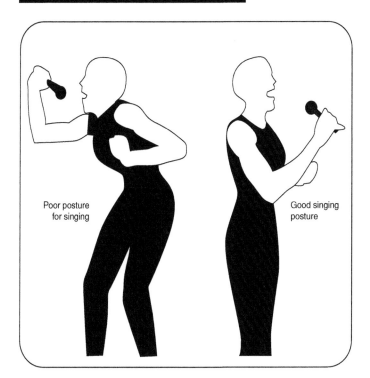

Poor posture for singing

Good singing posture

Breathing Exercises

Breath Observation

This exercise is helpful in encouraging proper abdominal action.

1. Lay on the floor and place a small book approximately 1 1/2 inches thick under your head.

2. Focus on your breathing. As you inhale, your abdominal muscles below your rib cage rise, and as you exhale, they move inward. Observe the openness of your ribs around your waist-line.

3. Rest your hands on your abdomen and breathe, observing the rise and fall of your belly.

4. Stand up, and reproduce this breathing action, expanding as you inhale.

Releasing Abdominal Muscles

This exercise will help you release the lower abdominal muscles to take a full breath.

Leaning Over a Table or Chair

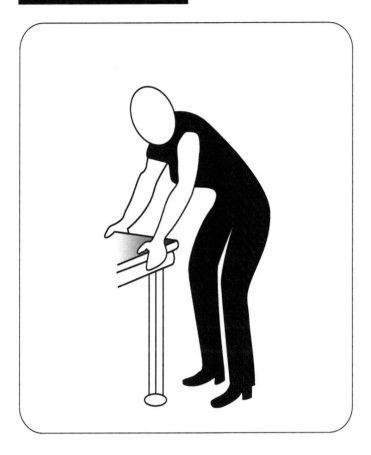

1. Stand with your feet about 18 inches away from a table (or the back of a chair).
2. Lean forward with your hands on the edge of the table.
3. Take a slow, deep breath, letting your belly fall toward the floor. Allow your abdominal muscles to drop.
4. Exhale, with firm abdominal muscles.
5. Inhale again, feeling the expansion in your back muscles and the release of your abdominal muscles.
6. Sing a few easy passages of a song, letting your abdominal muscles drop when you inhale.
7. Repeat steps 3–6, this time standing upright.

Extending Your Breath

This exercise can help coordinate and energize your breath support. Practice Step One until you can make it through comfortably, then add Step Two, then Step Three. Take care not to inhale too fast or raise your chest when you inhale. During exhalation, maintain the openness in your ribs for the entire count. When all three steps can be performed consecutively without stopping, increase the exhalation count to 25 or 30. Put your metronome on 80 b.p.m..

Step One

1. Inhale to a count of 10, taking in two tiny sips of air per metronome beat, expanding your lower abdominal muscles and ribs. Exhale for 20 beats using repeated short hisses, two hisses per metronome beat. After 20 counts, begin the next inhalation.

2. Inhale again to a count of 10, taking in two tiny sips of air per metronome beat. Exhale for 20 beats using one long, sustained hiss.

3. Inhale again to a count of 10, taking in two tiny sips of air per metronome beat. Sing "ah" on a comfortable pitch for 20 beats. Maintain the openness in your ribs. (Continue, without stopping, to Step Two if you successfully complete this with no problem.)

Step Two

1. Inhale to a count to 10, taking in one long, continuous, slow breath. Exhale for 20 beats using repeated short hisses, two hisses per metronome beat.

2. Inhale again to a count of 10 in a slow, continuous sip. Exhale in a slow continuous hiss to a count of 20.

3. Inhale again to a count of 10 in a slow, continuous sip. Sing "ah" on a comfortable pitch for 20 beats. Try to maintain the feeling of openness in your ribs for the entire exhalation. (Continue without stopping to Step Three if you successfully complete the first two steps.)

Step Three

1. Inhale in a quick catch breath in one count. Exhale for 20 beats using repeated short hisses, two hisses per metronome beat.
2. Inhale in a quick catch breath in one count. Exhale for 20 beats in a continuous hiss.
3. Inhale in a quick catch breath in one count. Sing "ah" for 20 beats.

Practice Routine

An organized practice routine helps you achieve more because you stay mentally focused and waste less time. If you follow a routine daily, you will find that you look forward to your practice time and gain the benefits of daily vocal exercise.

Tips for Productive Practice

Location. Work where you can relax and not be self-conscious. You need to feel free to make mistakes, and not hold back for fear of disturbing neighbors or family. If there is no place at home to practice, inquire at a local school or house of worship to see if there is a room that you could use regularly.

Keyboard/Guitar. Wherever you practice, you will need some kind of keyboard or guitar for checking pitches.

Mirror. Practice in front of a mirror, focusing on your body, posture, and expression. Observe tension in the face, neck, and jaw, which indicates a problem. Use the mirror to help correct awkward or tense looking movements. The muscles of your throat can become tight to compensate for a collapsed chest posture. Align your body in order to allow the muscles of your throat to function freely.

Tape Recorder. To hear a realistic (though imperfect) representation of your voice, use a cassette recorder in practice and at your voice lessons. You can learn a lot from hearing your own singing. Try to listen objectively, and don't be distracted from your goals by being overly critical.

Metronome. A metronome will help you establish and maintain tempos when working on songs and keep you from rushing when practicing scales.

Practice Routine
  I. Beginning Warm-up

   a. Physical Stretches (2–3 minutes)

   b. Warm-up Vocalizations (3–5 minutes)

  II. Vocal Technique (10–20 minutes)

  III. Song Study (15–20 minutes)

  IV. Cool Down (2–5 minutes)

I. Beginning Warm-up

You probably wouldn't run a couple of miles before warming up and stretching. In the same way, it is advisable to warm up vocally before working on vocal technique or songs. The equivalent of stretching your legs before you run, vocal warm-ups increase the blood flow to your muscles and gradually release tension to prepare your body for activity. The few minutes of physical stretches and warm-up vocalizations recommended here are intended to prepare your voice for more activity and are generally not enough to completely warm up your instrument. For a more comprehensive warm-up, complete the beginning warm-up and the vocal technique segment of this recommended practice routine.

A. Physical Stretches (2–3 minutes)

It is important to begin singing with physical freedom. We sing and perform with our entire bodies, which need to be prepared for activity.

Notes on warm-ups:

1. If you feel pain, stop immediately.
2. Don't hold your breath while stretching.
3. A stretched muscle is in a weakened position, so don't stress it by forcing or bouncing.
4. Read the directions for each exercise thoroughly before attempting it.
5. Choose a few of the following stretches. Do only what feels right and good to you. Listen to your body and use common sense.
6. Modify stretches to suit your needs and physical limitations.

Gentle Head Rolls

Purpose: to stretch the strong muscles of the neck and to release tension.

Let your jaw hang loose and open throughout this stretch. Go at your own pace, circling your head in both directions. If you become dizzy, keep your eyes open.

1. Gently drop your head so your chin is close to your chest, and let the weight of your head stretch the strong muscles of your neck. Do not push your head down—let it hang.

2. Starting from this position, slowly roll your head around until your right ear is close to your right shoulder.

3. Continue rolling your head until you're looking upward, elongating your spine, letting your mouth and jaw hang open. Avoid dropping your head all the way back, which would stress your neck muscles.

4. Continue the head roll circle until your left ear is near your left shoulder, pausing to stretch your neck.

In a continuous, slow movement, roll your head through each of these positions: chin to chest, ear to shoulder, eyes upward, and ear to shoulder. If your feel tension in a particular spot, pause and let the weight of your head stretch it out before continuing. Complete two or three full rotations and then reverse direction.

Neck Tension Releaser

Purpose: to release tension in neck muscles that may inhibit free laryngeal function in singing.

Your neck muscles are complex and can be susceptible to injury if you force your head into any position. Be gentle with this exercise, and use common sense.

1. Lean your right ear to your right shoulder and feel the weight of your head elongate the muscles on the side of your neck.

2. Reach your right arm over the top of your head and rest your right palm on your left ear, simply letting the weight of your arm increase the stretch in your neck muscles. Do not pull your head.

3. After you have stretched sufficiently (10–30 seconds), move your arm from your ear and just let your head hang in this position for a few seconds.

4. Next, support your head with your right hand, using it to bring it back to its upright position. To avoid stressing the stretched muscle, don't use your neck muscles alone to pull up your head. Repeat on your left side.

Shoulder Rolls

Purpose: to release tension in the upper back and shoulders.

Proceed at a slow, relaxed pace, moving from one position to the next without stopping. Focus on using a full range of motion. Remember to breathe normally.

1. Bring both shoulders up to your ears, then roll them back so your shoulder blades almost touch in back.

2. Bring them down to a relaxed position, and then forward to round your upper back.

3. Reverse directions, and roll in a continuous motion.

Rib Stretch

Purpose: to stretch and develop awareness of the rib muscles, and improve fullness of breath.

Rib stretches help release tension and prepare your body for the extended breathing used in singing.

1. Stand with your feet about shoulder-width apart.

2. Reach up with your right arm, palm flat to the ceiling, and stretch it upward and over the top of your head a bit, leaning to your left.

3. To increase this stretch, bend your right knee as you stretch your right arm up (your left leg should remain straight). You should feel a good stretch in your right-side rib muscles.

4. Repeat this stretch on your left side.

Full Roll-Down

Purpose: to increase awareness of abdominal and rib expansion during breathing and stretch your back, leg, and postural muscles to release tension.

When you are bent over at the waist, keep your knees loose (not locked), and only bend over as far as it feels comfortable. Do not force your palms to touch the floor.

1. Standing with feet hip-distance apart, slowly drop your chin to your chest. Continue to roll down, leading with your head, proceeding one vertebra at a time until you are bending over at the waist.

2. In this position, take a full breath that expands your belly and ribs. (The belly expansion will make you rise from the floor slightly.) Then exhale. Check the back of your neck to make sure you are not lifting your head, but rather letting the top of your head drop to the floor.

3. Still in this rolled-down position, breathe normally as you slightly bend and straighten your knees a few times, feeling the stretch in the back of your legs.

4. Shift your weight back slightly, so your hips are over your feet. With slightly bent knees, take one more breath, exhale, and slowly roll up one vertebra at a time, sensing your feet push into the floor. This action will help you use your legs to stand up again, instead of your newly stretched back muscles.

Chewing

Purpose: to induce relaxation in the facial muscles and free your jaw.

Stand or sit in a comfortable, relaxed position and imagine the sensation of your head floating effortlessly toward the ceiling.

1. Pretend you have two large pieces of bubble gum in your mouth, one on each side. Chew with exaggerated movements, with an open mouth, saying "mum-mum-mum."

2. Chew for a few seconds and rest. Do three or four repetitions of these exercises, then rest.

3. Sing or speak a line of text using the chewing action with vigorous movement of the lips, jaw, and cheeks. This exercise can be done in brief intervals throughout the day.

Self-Massage

Purpose: to release tension in your neck, facial muscles, and jaw.

You can target your own specific muscle tensions in this self-massage routine.

1. Standing or sitting comfortably and with your head level, massage the back and sides of your neck with the pads of your fingers in a gentle circular motion.

2. Work your fingers up the muscles in front of your ears and along the edge of your jaw.

3. Let your mouth drop open and massage in the soft spot directly under your chin with your thumbs.

4. Gently continue up the back of your neck to your head, place your fingers firmly on your scalp, and move your entire scalp around. Imagine air entering between your skull and your scalp.

5. End your massage by tracing long, firm strokes with your fingers along your eyebrows, one at a time, from the inside corner to the outside corner.

B. Warm-Up Vocalizations (3–5 minutes)

Sighs, humming, sliding, and lip trills are great for getting the "cobwebs" out and increasing blood flow to your vocal cords. Vocal slides and other nontraditional vocalizations like the ones suggested here allow your voice to function freely and prepare your voice for more vigorous activity.

Slides

Purpose: to begin vocalization exercises; useful especially for singers who are very tense.

During this exercise, check your jaw and neck for tension, and release it as you go. Explore the middle range of your voice, which should flow freely and have a consistent tone quality. Stand in front of a mirror, and begin to vocalize by sliding your voice up and down.

1. Start at or slightly above your speaking pitch and gently say, "hoo," letting your voice slide down in pitch in a slow, smooth descent. Imagine that you let the sound fall out of your body without trying to control or manipulate it.
2. Start at a slightly higher pitch and repeat.
3. Continue to a comfortably high level, and then proceed back down again.

Lip Trills

Purpose: to initiate tone production with a steady airflow and relaxed jaw.

Lip trills can be valuable at the start of a warm-up session, partly because they sound silly and help free you from inhibitions about singing. Practice to develop evenness in the trilling of your lips and in your tone quality. Don't be discouraged if at first you cannot make your lips bubble consistently. Many singers find that they can vocalize on a lip trill easier than on any other syllable. If this is true for you, take inventory of your vocal production, posture, and the sensations in your throat and neck when trilling. Evaluate how your voice feels and how you might develop the same sense of freedom singing on vowel sounds.

1. First try to make the sound of a motorboat by loosely bubbling your lips without any pitch. Let your jaw hang as if you have no control over the muscles in your mouth and tongue. Start by blowing air over the lips and letting them vibrate.
2. When this becomes consistent, add pitch. Slide freely through the middle range of your voice using a descending pattern.
3. If you have tried to make your lips trill without success, place your index fingers gently at each corner of your mouth. If this helps, vocalize lip trills with your fingers in this position. Take care not to slouch if you bring your hands to your mouth. If you still cannot do a lip trill, use the humming exercise instead.

Sliding Warm-Up

Combine sliding, which helps induce laryngeal relaxation and lip trills, to maintain a consistent airflow, for an effective beginning warm-up. Repeat the pattern moving up or down by half steps.

Humming

Purpose: to initiate tone production while increasing your awareness of forward resonance.

Light humming can be an ideal beginning vocalization because the buzzing sensation in your lips, mouth, and nose helps ensure correct natural tone placement.

1. Take a relaxed breath and lightly hum with your lips barely touching. The inside edges of your lips should buzz with vibrations.

2. As you continue to vocalize, first with descending slides, then with descending fifths pitched at the keyboard/guitar, try to feel the vibrations in your "mask."

Descending Hum/Slides

II. Vocal Technique (10–20 minutes)

This part of practicing will complete your warming up and help you work out vocally. During technique work, identify what you need to improve in your singing (increasing range, agility, breath control, improving tone quality). Regular vocal technique work will help keep your voice in shape, ready for the demands of singing. The purpose of technical work is to develop new skills and reinforce muscle memory. In singing, we learn by intellectually understanding concepts and by training muscles. It is both an intellectual and a physical process.

If you have skipped the beginning warm-up, I recommend that you back up and complete 2–3 minutes of light vocalizing first. Though many singers start practice by vocalizing scales, preceding vocal technique work with a beginning warm-up that includes physical stretches and easy vocalizing on a descending slide pattern is much more effective. If you are working on vocal flexibility and agility, for example, you may find that your voice feels sluggish and resistant to quick, light movements, if you have not warmed up. If you complete the recommended beginning warm-up, you can work more directly toward free, agile production and avoid the frustration of trying to sing before your voice is agile and your body is relaxed.

Identify your goals for your vocal technique practice. Have a purpose for every exercise or scale you sing. You can adapt exercises you know to suit your needs or make up your own exercises. Repeat the patterns, moving up by half steps.

Major/Minor Triplet for Flexibility

Extended Five-note Pattern for Flexibility and Breath

Two Fives and a Nine for Flexibility, Range, and Breath

Legato Flexibility Exercise

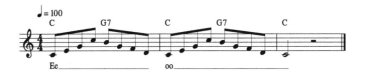

Long Tones for Vowel Equalization and Breath Extension

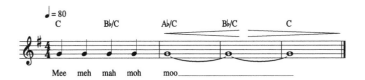

Octave Arpeggio for Range Extension and Flexibility

III. Song Study (15–20 minutes)

It requires flexibility to sing words and melody together, so after you have warmed up and worked out, your voice should be ready for the more demanding task of singing songs. Set aside this part of your practice routine to perfect notes and rhythms, study lyrics, add stylistic interpretation, and combine all these details into a technical and musical whole.

Seven Steps to Learning a New Song

1. Rhythm

Learn the notes and rhythms of your songs first. Take the time to read through the song rhythmically, and clap or say "tah" on the written rhythms. Use a metronome to maintain a steady beat. Though you may take liberties with written notes and rhythms, for expressive purposes, you need to know the original written notes and rhythms to see what the composer intended. Then you can develop your own interpretation.

2. Melody

After learning the rhythms, plunk out the melody on a keyboard or guitar. Learn the shape of the tune and review any tricky intervals. How does the melody lie in your voice? You should be able to sing through the song without straining. If the song feels too high or too low, experiment with different keys. Once you have decided on a key, you need written music or a lead sheet in that key. Do not ask an accompanist to transpose on sight during an audition or performance.

3. Rhythm and Melody Without Lyrics

Stand up, away from the pitched instrument, and sing your song in rhythm on a favorable vowel sound, but without the lyrics. Make the melody flow from note to note, observe dynamic markings, and check tricky rhythms and intervals. Plan where you will breathe, and work out your phrasing by marking (') in your music. If you've planned your phrasing well, you won't run out of air at the wrong times.

4. Add Basic Accompaniment

Sing the melody in rhythm on a favorable vowel with the accompaniment or basic chord changes. Don't skip this step. Never take a song into an audition or performance situation without first working with the accompaniment. It can change your entire concept of the melody and throw you off balance in the pressure of a performance situation.

5. Study the Lyrics

Look up words you don't understand, and look for underlying meaning in the text. Can you relate to it enough to give a good interpretation? Think of yourself as an actor interpreting dramatic text for an audience.

6. Listen to Recordings

Listen to recordings by other artists, and make observations that help you define your concept of a song. You can learn a great deal from recordings by observing the phrasing, tempo, rhythmic feel, and interpretation. How does the singer interpret the melody, rhythm, and harmony? Is the key of the song higher or lower than the key you are singing? Notice the singer's voice quality. Do you like it? Is the rhythmic feel or groove in the accompaniment what you imagined it would be like? How is it different from the printed music? What is the style the song (ballad, up-tempo, rock, jazz, Latin, etc.)? Answering these questions when you listen will help you fine-tune your concept of a song.

7. Interpret the Song

Add your own personal expression to a song. It can be in the way you deliver the lyrics, or if stylistically appropriate, changes to the melody or rhythm. It can include changes in specified dynamics, a different harmonization, addition or subtraction of vibrato in your voice, and experimentation with different vocal colors.

Study the lyrics. Understand what you are singing, and try to express the feelings and emotions of the lyrics to your audience. If you watch yourself in a mirror, you will see that subtle expression in your eyes can enhance your communication of a song.

IV. Cool Down (2–5 minutes)

It is as important to cool down vocally, after practice, to bring your vocal cords back to a less active state, so your speaking voice doesn't feel unstable. It is especially important to cool down if you are going out into cold weather, or if you have been singing high notes for a while.

To cool down, repeat the body and voice work of the beginning warm-up from the first part of your practice session. Are your shoulders or other parts of your body sore after practice? Stretch out physically, targeting the tension spots in your body. Lighter stretches can be combined with light humming or sighs, and you should also repeat some of the less intense technical exercises.

Mental Practicing

Mental practicing is rehearsing without using your voice. It can be used when you are vocally tired, ill, or when you are healthy but are not mentally focused enough on the tasks at hand. Mental practice not only rests your voice, but also can bring mental alertness back to a practice session and can be an effective method of problem solving. It can also be used to take a break from regular vocal practice to conserve your voice.

If you mentally practice a song with intensity, you can learn without actually singing. As we mentally practice, we actually produce muscle contractions (so small they cannot be felt) that are similar to the ones we produce when we perform. Try this guided imagery exercise to improve your mental focus.

Guided Imagery Exercise

Relax in a comfortable chair, and notice your breathing. It should be deep and relaxed. Imagine yourself in the place where you usually practice or perform. Imagine how quiet and peaceful the surroundings are. Now imagine the details: the floor, the height of the ceiling, the smell of the room, the temperature, the sound and feel of the place. Mentally go to the place in this room where you sing. Notice how your muscles feel as you prepare to sing. Take inventory of your body position in this imagined space, and feel the anticipation of the performance. Imagine yourself taking a deep breath and beginning your song, singing through each phrase flawlessly. In your imagery, you will always breathe in the right spots and sing the way you want. Proceed through your performance phrase by phrase, not skipping, but singing the song all the way through in your mind. Sing through the performance, feeling that you have done your best.

Repeat this exercise, emphasizing your awareness of sound and feel. It is important to see yourself succeed. Imagine your sense of pride in your accomplishment at the end of your mental practice. Sense the feel, sounds, and energy of a live audience. Imagine a positive audience reaction and your feeling of accomplishment.

Strong emotions are involved in the mental practice of correct vocal skills. During your guided imagery, if negative thoughts or mistakes creep into your thinking, stop the imagery, rewind it like a videotape in your mind, and proceed forward again in slow motion, frame by frame, seeing yourself execute the trouble spots easily, without any catches. Work through any negative thoughts and turn them into positive images.

Breathing for Relaxation

Breath is essential to making sound for singing. Concentrating on deep breathing before practice and performance will help relax your muscles and focus your mind. With a focused mind and relaxed body, you will be ready for singing. If you don't take the time to relax, you will find singing is much harder work. You may be fighting with residual tension and negative thoughts that prevent efficient muscle coordination.

Take a deep breath, imagining that you are filling up the bottom of your lungs first. Let your abdomen relax and ribs open. Breathe in through your nose and mouth. Your throat should feel relaxed. Your diaphragm will stretch downward and your abdomen should relax outward, allowing your lungs to expand. Let your ribs relax, and exhale all of your air. Draw your abdominal muscles in to completely empty your lungs.

Remember to inhale and think of relaxation, exhale and release any tension. Repeat this exercise several times over the course of the day to release tension and invigorate your body and mind. This exercise is specifically for releasing tension and improving mental focus. It is similar to the breath action used in singing, but in relaxation exercises, your rib muscles don't resist the action of your diaphragm during exhalation.

Think when you practice. Then allow yourself time to turn off your mind and just sing. Repetition will teach your muscles to remember how to do the things you've been practicing. Then let go.

Maintaining Your Vocal Health

If singers were to sing only when they feel completely health , and stress-free, many of us would never be able to make a living performing. That is why it is important to prevent problems by knowing yourself, your voice, your limits, and how to take care of yourself.

If singing hurts, don't sing.

Disregard for your vocal health and long rehearsals, combined with pressure from a music director or bandleader to rehearse songs repeatedly, can tire or strain your voice.

Pain in your larynx can be a sign of a problem. Singers experiencing pain, huskiness, or hoarseness and loss of high range should see a throat specialist (laryngologist) experienced in working with singers. Performing arts venues, music colleges, conservatories, and other singers can usually refer you to such a doctor. Often, general "ear, nose, and throat" doctors (otolaryngologists) do not have the specialized expertise in performing-arts medicine to optimally help vocalists.

Singers should watch for signs of vocal cord swelling, characterized by slight hoarseness or raspiness, a speaking voice that feels higher and huskier than normal, and a vocal quality that sounds coarse and less than clean. Frequently, there is a loss of high range, and you need more breath support than normal because of inefficient vocal cord vibrations. A virus can cause this type of problem, as can overuse of your voice.

If you have what seems to be more than a simple cold, consult a qualified specialist for advice and treatment.

Don't delay! Go to a laryngologist who works with singers. A skilled specialist will be more sensitive to your personal feelings about your singing. They can offer advice regarding any upcoming singing engagements.

Singing over a cold.

There are times when you can sing with a cold and times when you should rest your voice. When an occasional cold comes on, you can rely on breath support and body awareness to get through rehearsals and concerts without exacerbating fatigue or doing permanent damage.

You can usually sing over a cold if you have nasal congestion but no throat symptoms. The first line of treatment is moisture. Drink a lot of water to keep your vocal-tract mucus thin. Inhaling steam also seems to be helpful. Cough drops can help keep you from coughing, but the sugar and menthol in them can dry you out. Caffeine, alcohol, and smoking should be avoided because these are all drying to your voice and body. Herbal teas (caffeine-free) can be soothing and add moisture to your system.

Avoid sprays that numb throat pain. Throat pain indicates that you should not be singing. Singing while you are numbing your throat pain can be a recipe for problems. Consult your doctor for advice about the use of any medication.

Choose repertoire carefully, and avoid music that is taxing in range or intensity.

If you need to change the key of a song, do it. It is not an artistic compromise to transpose pop songs to a comfortable range. Extend your range with scale patterns and exercises. But recognize that some songs may not be right for your voice, no matter how much you like them.

Develop your own unique voice.

Study great singers, transcribe and sing great solos, listen to phrasing, and figure out what makes these singers unique. But it is not vocally healthy to imitate others to the exclusion of developing your own voice. Voices often don't fully mature until singers are in their mid-twenties or even into their thirties, so be patient and don't force your voice.

Pay attention to the way you speak.

Your instrument produces both your speaking and singing voice, so your singing can be negatively affected by poor speaking habits. To prevent this, employ touch-distance talking. Only speak to those who are within an arm's length, or touching distance, away. This will help you control the urge to shout and prevent unnecessary strain. Likewise, whispering is tiring to your vocal cords, so don't make the mistake of thinking it conserves your voice.

Avoid prolonged talking around noise, dust, and smoke.

Performing

Performing environments, such as theaters, clubs, and bars, are often dusty, smoky, and noisy—all things to be avoided by singers. To prevent vocal burnout:

- **Avoid smoky areas.**
- **Keep quiet on breaks.** Talking over background music and other noise makes you talk louder than normal and can lead to vocal strain.
- **Avoid alcohol and caffeine while performing.** Your vocal cords should be well lubricated for your voice to function best. Alcohol and caffeine dry your body and vocal mechanism; avoid them when performing. Alcohol can also limit your judgment about how loud you are singing, impair your ability to sing in tune, and lead to unnecessary strain. Drinks containing alcohol and caffeine can also lead to reflux laryngitis.

Traveling

In cars, airplanes, trains, and other vehicles, background noise forces you to speak louder than normal, which can be detrimental to your voice.

- **Airplanes.** The air on planes is typically very dry and recycled throughout the plane—conditions that dehydrate the vocal mechanism and body. Responding to a talkative seatmate on a long flight can wear out your voice. Drinking alcohol can compound this wear and tear. Before traveling, prepare your body by super-hydrating, drinking eight to ten glasses of water a day for several days beforehand.

- **Cars.** Background noise makes you have to sing louder to hear yourself. Your posture is compromised by the car seat, so you are not as likely to support your voice adequately. It is more productive to practice in a place where you can really hear yourself and concentrate on what you are doing.

Avoid throat clearing.

Throat clearing is hard to avoid when you have a stubborn spot of thick mucus rattling around and you're trying to sing. But when you clear your throat, you not only remove the bothersome mucus, you can irritate the leading edges of your vocal cords. This makes your body produce more mucus to protect them, and it becomes a circular problem. When practicing, try to sing the mucus off. If you must clear your throat, do it gently, and avoid habitual throat clearing.

If you have severe coughing spasms caused by bronchial irritation, see a doctor. You might benefit from medication that controls coughing, thereby minimizing irritation to your vocal cords. A doctor's treatment may also involve antibiotics, reflux treatment, or mucus-thinning medications. Be aware that many over-the-counter decongestants have the tendency to dry out your vocal cords.

Develop good rehearsal habits.

Warming up before rehearsals will help you avoid strain. During a long rehearsal, take breaks, drink plenty of water, and use a well-positioned monitor that lets you hear yourself sing with an amplified band. Do not schedule a long rehearsal the evening before or the day of a performance; this can take the freshness out of your voice.

Stay physically fit.

Your body is your instrument. Whatever you do to improve the health of your body and mind eventually shows up in your voice as increased vitality and energy. Singing is physically demanding, and maintaining good health is essential to success. Physical exercise can help you stay physically and mentally alert, as well as have more energy.

Drink water.

Drink six to eight 8 oz. glasses of water per day. This can help your voice function better because your vocal cords must be well lubricated to vibrate without too much friction. The water you drink does not go immediately to your vocal cords. Although you feel the immediate relief of water in your throat, water goes to your stomach and passes through your entire system before hydrating your vocal cords. It takes time for this to happen, so be sure to drink water before you feel thirsty.

Drinks with alcohol and caffeine may contain water but should not be counted toward your daily water intake because of their drying effect on your body.

Eat well-balanced meals.

Eat lightly and well in advance of a performance. Large amounts of food and liquid take up space in your body and may interfere with breath management. Milk products can cause excessive mucus production and should be avoided before singing, if they affect you adversely.

Reflux occurs when the contents of your stomach migrate back into the esophagus and throat, causing inflammation. Singers sensitive to reflux react to a number of foods and drinks that can impact their vocal condition and singing by causing reflux laryngitis. Singers are particularly prone to reflux due to the high abdominal pressure that is used in breath support.

Dr. Steven Zeitels, director of the Division of Laryngology at the Massachusetts Eye and Ear Infirmary in Boston, notes that most individuals with laryngeal reflux do not have heartburn, as is commonly thought. Reflux increases the mucus production often associated with throat clearing, produces an ill-defined feeling of fullness in the throat, and can cause hoarseness, chronic coughing, and difficulty in swallowing. Consuming soda, citrus, spicy foods, caffeine, and alcohol can precipitate and aggravate reflux. Singers should consult with a laryngologist if this is suspected to be a problem.

Eating disorders such as bulimia and anorexia plague many people, especially women, and can ruin your voice and health. In a music career, appearance can be considered very important and singers sometimes take desperate measures. Laxative abuse, bingeing and purging, starving, and abusing weight-loss drugs can sap your vitality and strength. Repeated vomiting erodes the lining of your throat and mouth and irritates your throat. Because these urges can become uncontrollable and seriously affect your health, if you think you have an eating disorder, get professional help.

Get plenty of rest.

Know how much sleep you need and maintain a regular sleep schedule. Rest your voice whenever possible. Schedule time to unwind during your day. Don't wait until you burn out before you schedule down-time away from stressful activities.

If you sing with an amplified band, always use a microphone.

Singers who cannot hear themselves tend to compensate by over-singing. This is a sure way to wear out your voice. Use a microphone when singing with an amplified band. Position yourself so you can hear your voice from an amp or monitor.

Keep your microphone in a separate bag that's easy to locate. All you have to do is grab it and go. In addition to your microphone, it should contain a mic cord and XLR-to-1/4 inch transformer for connecting to a guitar or keyboard amp. Find out about the sound system, monitor, and other equipment in the performance space so you will know what to bring.

Pay attention to common medications, including contraceptive pills.

Only a trained doctor or voice specialist can evaluate your need for medications. Ask your doctor about prescription and nonprescription medications and their effects on your voice. Antihistamines, aspirin, and other common medicines can affect your vocal health.

In some women, birth control pills affect the mass of the vocal cords, resulting in less flexibility and loss of high range. The levels of hormones in these drugs vary according to brand and dosage, as does their effect on individual women's voices. If you are already taking birth control pills and experience changes in your voice, consult your doctor. However, it is best to consult a laryngologist before beginning these medications.

Do not smoke.

Any singer who is serious about having a career in music should not smoke. Smoking has long been known to cause emphysema and cancer of the mouth and vocal tract. It irritates vocal tract membranes and your vocal cords. When these membranes are dry and irritated from the chemicals in smoke, your body tries to compensate with secretions. These make you need to clear your throat, which causes further irritation.

> **Take care of yourself.**
> Eat a variety of healthful foods, including whole grains, fruits, and vegetables.
>
> Get enough sleep at regular hours.
>
> Stick to a moderate exercise routine.
>
> Wash your hands with soap and warm water frequently.
>
> Drink six to eight 8 oz. glasses of water each day.

You only have one voice.

Some singers seem to be able to scream constantly and still sustain a successful career in rock music. Others can have a single incident of voice abuse and end up with vocal cord nodules.

The limits of safe vocal use vary greatly from person to person. Learn what it takes for your voice to be in peak shape and ready to sing. Learn what triggers stress for you; it can sap your energy and make you susceptible to illness. Know your tendencies for talking too much, drinking, and other excesses. Self-knowledge is one of the keys to maintaining your voice.

Some singers purposely try to add huskiness to their voices by screaming, smoking, or drinking. Such singers can end up with no voice at all. Tearing down your voice is not the way to add character. Instead, build it by learning how to sing and exploring all the possibilities of your instrument. Gain performance experience and interpret your songs with sincere emotion, rather than manipulating your voice in a way that can permanently damage and limit your vocal possibilities.

Possible Causes of Vocal Maladies

Many factors can contribute to the development of vocal cord nodules, polyps, and chronic laryngitis. The list below shows some of the possible causes of and contributing factors to these serious vocal maladies.

Non-singing Factors

Shouting, screaming, and yelling, including cheerleading.

Poor speaking habits.

Repeated straining, as when lifting heavy objects.

Talking over background noise at concerts and clubs, or in airplanes and cars.

Making odd noises with your voice.

Reflux.

Smoking.

Excessive coughing and habitual throat clearing.

Excessive dryness of the vocal mechanism caused by your environment, lack of adequate hydration, medications, or over-consumption of alcohol and/or caffeine.

Singing Factors

Not warming up.

Singing at the extremes of your range for long periods.

Imitating other singers to the exclusion of developing your own voice.

Singing without adequate amplification.

Insufficient breath support.

Pushing your voice when overtired or sick.

Overusing your voice.

35

Marking for Voice Conservation

Marking is a way of singing that helps you save your voice during rehearsals. To mark a melody, sing just the first few notes of a phrase, and mentally sing the other notes. Raise the lowest and lower the highest notes in your song by an octave (octave displacement) to avoid the extremes of your range. Men can use falsetto to approach high notes. All singing should be light when you are marking.

Marking saves your voice by minimizing its use. It should be used when you are not feeling well, or during rehearsals scheduled just before a performance. Too much practicing before a performance can take the freshness out of your voice. In theater music, singers mark during lighting and technical rehearsals, when it is not important for them to sing at full volume.

Singers often have strong emotions when performing and become carried away by the moment, losing self-control and singing full voice when they should be resting, so listen to your body.

What to Do When Marking

1. Warm up lightly first.
2. Maintain energetic breath support.
3. Sing only the first few words of a phrase, singing the rest mentally.
4. Displace notes at the high and low extremes of your range by an octave to avoid straining. Plan this in advance.
5. Men can sing high notes in falsetto when marking.
6. Always sing lightly when marking.

What to Avoid When Marking

1. Don't sing everything down an octave.
2. Don't whisper or withhold breath support.
3. Don't lose concentration.
4. Don't succumb to pressure from peers or directors and sing full voice against the advice of your doctor.
5. Don't mark all of the time. You should sing a concert, recital, or other long performance using your full voice several times over a period of several weeks or longer to make sure you are familiar with phrasing and breath pacing, and to help you develop stamina.

About the Author

Anne Peckham is a singer, voice teacher, and author. A professor in the Voice Department at Berklee College of Music, Anne teaches private voice lessons, directs Berklee's Musical Theater Workshop, and has developed curriculum for "Elements of Vocal Technique," a required course for all of Berklee's vocal students. Anne is the author of The Contemporary Singer, a book/CD set published by Berklee Press. The Contemporary Singer has recently been released in a Japanese translation.

A member of the National Association of Teachers of Singing, Anne served as vice president of the board of directors of the association's Boston chapter, and co-chaired the chapter's annual Song Festival. She frequently appears as a clinician and adjudicator for choral and song festivals in the U.S., Europe, and Canada.

Anne sang with the Tanglewood Festival Chorus for four years, performing on two recordings with the Boston Pops, including a featured solo in their televised Gilbert and Sullivan presentation that aired on PBS. She has performed with regional theater companies, was the principal section leader at the Congregational Church of Needham for eleven years, and performs frequently in recital and cabaret venues.